PEACE ON EARTH TO MEN OF GOOD WILL

Peace
Not as the World Gives

*Consoling thoughts on Divine
Providence and Conformity
to the Will of God*

Compiled and Edited by
Fr. F. X. Lasance

The Neumann Press
Long Prairie, Minnesota 56347

Nihil Obstat
> ARTHUR J. SCANLAN, S.T.D.
> *Censor Librorum*

Imprimatur
> PATRICK CARDINAL HAYES
> *Archbishop of New York*
>
> New York, March 23, 1938

© 1990 The Neumann Press
Printed and Published in the United States of America by
The Neumann Press, Long Prairie, Minnesota 56347

To

MARY IMMACULATE
OUR LADY OF GRACE

CONTENTS

	PAGE
Peace, the Gift of the Infant Jesus	9
Heart of Jesus, Our Peace and Reconciliation	11
Christmas	17
Peace with God	20
Peace with Our Neighbor	21
Peace with Oneself	22
Peace of Heart	24
Peace Is Found in Conformity to the Will of God	25
Thy Will Be Done	27
Gethsemani	33
The Will of God	37
What Madness!	39
The Infinite Wisdom of God	40
Trust in God	42
God Hath Care of You	43
Requiescant in Pace	46
Heaven, Our Home	49
The Providence of God	53
The Loving Dispensations of Divine Providence	57
Along the Royal Road	63
Tranquillity	64
The Weather	66
St. Francis de Sales	67

	PAGE
Tribulations	69
The Path of Perfection	71
An Act of Abandonment	78
An Act of Confidence in God	79
Blessed Are the Peacemakers	81
Peace in Absolute Surrender to Divine Providence	85
Indulgenced Ejaculation of Resignation to the Will of God	96
A Plenary Indulgence at the Hour of Death	96
Prayer for Perseverance	97
Peace of Mind	98
Adversities	98
Remain Tranquil	102
Peace of Soul after a Fault	103
My Peace I Give unto You	106
The Peace of God *(Poem)*	109
Life, a Continual Prayer	112
Heaven	113
Suffering	116
Our Eternal Home	117
Trust and Rest *(Poem)*	118
A Great Secret for Preserving Peace of Heart	119
One Little Secret of a Happy Life	121
Stay with Me, Lord *(Poem)*	123
An Act of Confidence in God	125
An After-Thought *(Poem)*	128

PEACE, THE GIFT OF THE INFANT JESUS

Glory to God in the highest, and on earth peace to men of good will. This was the song of the angels in the Holy Night. Peace, the gift which the divine Child brought with Him from above, will not be bestowed on those individuals who are endowed with a good understanding or a good memory; it will not be granted to those who excel in bodily strength, who are remarkable for their personal beauty or for their noble birth; it will be given solely and exclusively to the men of good will, no matter if all else be lacking to them—intellectual superiority; distinguished beauty, a splendid physique, high position. And who is the man of good will? He who desires and asks and strives after nothing else but solely and wholly what God wills. He is a man of good will who is no less ready to drink vinegar and gall, if such be the Lord's will, than to accept with gratitude for his consolation the most costly and delicious wine, if God presents it to him; who is equally willing to have a crown of thorns pressed on to his head, as to wear a regal crown of gold, since he is actuated in either case only by the love of God. Alas, my soul, how far you fall short of being a man of good will; how far you are from being able to take as your motto the beautiful words: "What Thou willest, Lord, as Thou willest, as long as Thou willest, and because Thou willest it." How far are you from resembling St. Stephen, who was the first to make manifest his good will, that is, the complete conformity of his will to the will of God, by gladly offering to God the sacrifice of his life; who, whilst he was being stoned, repeated, in deed at least if not in word, the prayer his Lord uttered: "Not my will, but Thine be done."

* * *

Solomon, having prayed for wisdom, received every other good thing along with it; and we too, if, like good Christians, we leave ourselves in our heavenly Father's hands and have no other wish but to please Him, shall most certainly have many temporal blessings poured out upon us. God will never send us a life wholly free from suffering, for that is not the way to heaven; but He will give us peace, that peace which surpasseth all understanding, leading through storm and sunshine to eternal joy. "Peace I leave with you. My peace I give unto you; not as the world giveth do I give unto you" (John xiv. 27).

HEART OF JESUS, OUR PEACE AND RECONCILIATION

The peace of our soul depends on the proper observance of four sets of relations—i.e., with *God,* by love and conformity to His divine will, with *men,* by justice and charity; with *ourselves,* by the due subordination of the body to the soul, of the inferior appetites to reason; with *inferior creatures,* by making them subservient to our last end. The better we observe these four relations, the greater our peace of soul. In heaven alone shall we enjoy this peace in its perfection. On earth, even its imperfect possession is an unspeakable blessing, the nearest approach to true happiness. Again and again Christ wished it to His disciples: *"Pax vobis"* (Peace be to you) was His frequent form of address. "Peace I leave you, My peace I give unto you. . . . Let not your heart be troubled, nor let it be afraid." (John xiv. 27.) "Learn of Me . . . and you will find rest to your souls." (Matt. xi. 29.) The Church in its Liturgy prays again and again for peace.) "May the peace of the Lord be always with you."

Now, the Sacred Heart is called "our peace and reconciliation" in the same sense as, in another invocation, it is called "our life and

HEART OF JESUS, OUR PEACE AND RECONCILIATION

resurrection"—*viz.*, the Sacred Heart is the cause of our peace and reconciliation. "He is our peace," says St. Paul (Eph. ii. 14) ". . . that He might reconcile" us to God. This peace-making influence of the Saviour we attribute to His Sacred Heart.

Our "peace and reconciliation" are the direct result of the shedding of the precious blood, which has its source and well-spring in the Sacred Heart; moreover, the work of pacification and reconciliation is peculiarly the outcome of the love, and therefore of the Heart, of the Redeemer.

The one, great, everlasting longing of the Sacred Heart is our "reconciliation" with His Father and our final admission to the everlasting bliss of heaven. For this He lived on earth, for this He died, for this He dwells throughout the ages in the tabernacle.*

Peace, says St. Augustine, is serenity of mind, tranquillity of soul, simplicity of heart, the bond of charity.

SERENITY OF MIND

Our mind is like the sky, that may be either resplendent with sunshine or darkened with

---

* Rev. Joseph McDonnell, S.J., *Commentary and Meditations on The Litany of the Sacred Heart.*

clouds. The clouds are gloomy thoughts, rash judgments, suspicions, uncharitable feelings—all, in short, that destroys interior peace.

TRANQUILLITY OF SOUL

Our tranquillity is disturbed by thoughts about the past—its faults, failures, and mishaps; the present—its troubles and sorrows; the future—its possibilities and apprehensions. The remedy for all this is confidence in God, conformity to His holy will, abandonment to the guidance and protection of Providence.

SIMPLICITY OF HEART

This may be defined as an active spirit of faith, which makes us simple, sincere, and straightforward in our relations with God and with our neighbor.

THE BOND OF CHARITY

To have peace of heart there must be charity in *thought*—avoiding envy, suspicion, jealousy, and all that embitters the mind; in *word*—avoiding calumny, detraction, unkindness of speech; in *action*—by being kindly and thoughtful in act toward others, even generous and self-sacrificing at times, and free from selfishness.

All these things we shall find in Him who was "meek and humble"; who came to give 'peace on earth to men of good will'"; and who so often invoked the sweet blessing of peace on His disciples of old.

PRAYER FOR PEACE

Give peace, O Lord, in our days; for there is none other that fighteth for us, but only Thou, our God.

V. Let there be peace in Thy strength, O Lord.

R. And plenty in Thy strong places.

Let us pray

O God, from Whom proceed all holy desires, all right counsels and just works; grant unto us Thy servants that peace which the world cannot give, that our hearts may be devoted to Thy service and that, being delivered from the fear of our enemies, we may pass our time in peace under Thy protection. Through Christ our Lord. Amen.

Indulgence: 100 days, every time.—Pius IX, May 18, 1848.

PRAYER FOR FIDELITY AND CONFORMITY TO THE DIVINE WILL

O Lord almighty, Who permittest evil to draw good therefrom, hear our humble prayers, and grant that we remain faithful to Thee unto death. Grant us also, through the intercession of most holy Mary, the strength ever to conform ourselves to Thy most holy will.

Indulgence: 100 days, once a day.—Pius IX, June 15, 1862; Leo XIII, July 19, 1879.

CHRISTMAS

All the world was at peace at the moment when Christ was born. The angry passions of men were hushed, as if in compliment to the *Prince of Peace.* He never comes where strife and confusion prevail. If I desire that He should come into my heart, I must resolve to keep under my evil passions and the self-will that dares to do battle against the will of God.

On the night of the Nativity a countless multitude of the heavenly host were singing the praises of the new-born King. Let us listen to them.

They are singing *Gloria in excelsis Deo*—"Glory to God in the highest!" It is the first song they have sung on earth since the Fall. It is sung on the occasion of the infinite humiliation of the Son of God. Yet they sing "Glory to God in the highest!" It must therefore be a source of unspeakable glory to God that He has taken the form of a servant, that He has humbled Himself to the very dust. If this is such a source of glory to God, my true glory must consist in humbling myself.

They are also singing of peace to me. What sort of peace? True peace, internal peace, that tranquillity of soul that nothing can destroy. This is the boon that Christ gives to all who love Him, in proportion to their love.

Peace, not for all, but for men of good will. Christ indeed brought peace to all, but all did not accept it—only those whose good will and loyal spirit of submission made them ready to acknowledge Him as their Lord, and whom, therefore, the good will of God had predestined to the eternal peace and joy of heaven God grant that I may be one of these!

The first who came to pay their homage to the new-born King were the shepherds who were watching in the fields of Bethlehem, and to whom an Angel had announced the birth of Christ the Lord. They received this honor because

They were poor, and therefore were well suited to gather round the King who came to live in poverty on earth. The eternal Father chose poverty for His well-beloved Son, and therefore poverty must be better than riches. The poor are to be envied rather than pitied, so long as their poverty is not due to their own sin or folly. How many who have saved their souls in poverty would have lost them if they had been rich! Hence, if you are poor do not regret your poverty, but rather rejoice in it.

They were simple of heart, untainted by

the world's deceits. None but good, simple men would have thus come in the darkness of the night to the stable of Bethlehem to find their Saviour and their King. God loves simplicity. "If thine eye be single, thy whole body shall be lightsome," says Our Lord; and He thereby describes the happy lot of those whose one aim is to do their work with simplicity for God alone. Is this my spirit?

They were shepherds. The occupation is one which God seems to love. The man after God's own heart was a shepherd. Our Lord calls Himself the Good Shepherd. Every Christian is a shepherd, in that some sheep or lambs are committed to his care. Am I a zealous shepherd of the sheep of Christ?

* * *

Better is a man that hath less wisdom, and wanteth understanding, with the fear of God, than he that aboundeth in understanding and transgresseth the law of the Most High.—
—*Ecclus., xix. 21.*

Jesus, calling unto Him a little child, set him in the midst of them, and said: Amen, I say to you, unless you be converted and become as little children, you shall not enter into the kingdom of heaven. Whosoever, therefore, shall humble himself as this little child, he is the greater in the kingdom of heaven. —*Matt. xviii, 2-4*

PEACE WITH GOD

Reflect that as Our Saviour, the night before His passion, bequeathed His peace to His disciples, saying: "Peace I leave with you; My peace I give unto you," so also after His resurrection, on three occasions He wished them His peace, saying: "Peace be to you." But what kind of peace is this that He so much inculcates and so earnestly desires to impart to us? Not the peace which the world pretends to give, which is false and deceitful like itself, they say, *"Peace, peace, and there is no peace"* (Ezech. xiii. 10), but *"the peace of God which surpasseth all understanding"* (Philipp. iv. 7). A threefold peace; namely, a peace of the soul with God, a peace with every neighbor, and a peace with oneself. And first, whosoever desires any degree of happiness, either here or hereafter, must take care to keep an inviolable peace with God, by ever flying wilful sin, which is at enmity with God. For how can there be any good for them that are at war with God. 'Who hath ever resisted Him and hath had peace?" (Job. ix. 4). "The wicked are like the raging sea, which cannot rest, and the waves thereof cast up dirt and mire: there is no peace to the wicked, saith the Lord God" (Is. lvii. 20, 21).

PEACE WITH OUR NEIGHBOR

Reflect that the Christian cannot maintain his peace with God if he does not also *'follow peace with all men"* (Heb. xi. 14); *"and as much as lies in him, keep peace with all men"* (Rom. xii. 18). *"For as no man can love God that does not love his neighbor"* (1 John iv.), so no man can be at peace with God that breaks peace with his neighbor.

It is, then, another branch both of the duty and of the happiness of a Christian to be at peace with every man, at least as far as lies in his power; to renounce all animosity and rancor, all discord and contention, all malice and envy, and whatsoever else is opposite to fraternal charity, and to learn to *bear*, and to *forbear*, which are the two great means of keeping peace with our neighbors: when on our part we forbear giving them any offense or provocation, either by word or deed, and at the same time bear with Christian meekness and charity all the offenses or provocations we receive at their hands, and strive to overcome them by rendering good for evil. Oh, how much happier is such a soul than one that is always at war with one neighbor or another, and always in a storm at home in his own interior!

PEACE WITH ONESELF

Another necessary branch of the Christian's peace is, to be at peace within himself, by striving to banish from his own interior whatsoever may disturb the tranquillity of his soul. This inward peace, when it is perfect, is a certain foretaste of heaven; it is a kind of heaven; it is a kind of heaven upon earth. In such souls God is pleased to dwell, of whom the Royal Prophet sings (Ps. lxxv.), that "His place is in peace, and His abode in Sion." To come at this happy peace (besides taking care to keep peace with God by a clean conscience, and with every neighbor by concord and charity), we must have our passions mortified, our affections well ordered and regulated, and our desires restrained; we must banish all hurry and overeagerness; all sadness and melancholy; all scrupulous fears, anxious cares, and uneasiness about the things of this world; and, above all things and in all things, we must conform ourselves to the holy will of God. Practise these lessons, my soul, and thou wilt be at peace, at least as far as the condition of thy mortal pilgrimage will allow of.

Conclude ever to aim at this threefold peace, with thy God, with thy neighbor, and with thyself; pray daily for it; and whatsoever fear, affection, or desire, or any other thing whatsoever offers to disturb thy heart, shut the door against it as an enemy, as a messenger of Satan, who comes to rob thee of thy treasure, the peace of thy soul.

PEACE WITH JESUS IN THE SACRAMENT OF HIS LOVE

Sweet Jesus! by this Sacrament of Love
All gross affections from my heart remove;
Let but Thy loving kindness linger there,
Preserved by grace and perfected by prayer;
And let me to my neighbor strive to be
As mild and gentle as Thou art with me.
Take Thou the guidance of my whole career,
That to displease Thee be my only fear;
Give me that peace the world can never give,
And in Thy loving presence let me live.
Ah! show me always, Lord, Thy holy will
And to each troubled thought say,
"Peace, be still."

PEACE OF HEART

A great secret for preserving peace of heart is to do nothing with over-eagerness, but to act always calmly, without trouble or disquiet. We are not asked to do much, but to do well. At the Last Day, God will not examine if we have performed a multitude of works, but if we have sanctified our souls in doing them. Now, the means of sanctifying ourselves is to do everything for God and to do perfectly whatever we have to do. The works that have as their motive vanity or selfishness make us neither better nor happier, and we shall receive no reward for them.

Patience hath a perfect work; that you may be perfect, failing in nothing.

—James i. 4.

Whatsoever you do in word or in work, do all in the name of the Lord Jesus Christ.

—Col. iii. 17.

PEACE IS FOUND IN CONFORMITY TO THE WILL OF GOD

God desires only that which is best for us, namely, our sanctification. "This is the will of God," says the Apostle, "your sanctification" (Thess. iv. 3). Let us take care, therefore, to subdue our own will, uniting it always to the will of God; and thus also let us endeavor to control our mind, reflecting that everything that God does is best for us. Whoever does not act thus, will never find true peace. All the perfection which can be attained in this world, which is a place of purification, and consequently a place of troubles and afflictions, consists in suffering patiently those things which are opposed to our self-love; and in order to suffer them with patience, there is no more efficacious means than a willingness to suffer them in order to do the will of God. Submit thyself then to Him, and be at peace" (Job xxii. 21). He that acquiesces with the divine will in everything, is always at peace; and nothing of all that happens to him can make him unhappy. "Whatever shall befall the just man, it shall not make him sad" (Prov. xii. 21). But why is the just man never miserable in any circumstances? Because he knows well, that whatever happens in the world, happens through the will of God.

—*St. Alphonsus Liguori.*

* * *

We deceive ourselves greatly if we think that union with God consists in ecstasies and spiritual consolations. It consists alone in thinking, saying, doing that which is in conformity to the will of God. This union is perfect when our will is detached from everything, attached but to God in such a manner that it breathes but His pure will. This is the true and essential union that I ardently desire, and continually ask of Our Lord.

—*St. Teresa.*

THY WILL BE DONE

When they had sung a hymn after the Last Supper, Jesus and His disciples went forth to the Mount of Olives. It is with hearts full of fear and foreboding that the apostles follow Him; for the cross has now for the first time cast its shadow upon their path, that cross which has been resting its whole weight on the heart of Our Saviour from His childhood upward. And Jesus saith to them: All you shall be scandalized in Me this night." Their hearts are brimful of love for Him now! yet He foresees sadly how their human frailty will give way under the awful trial about to fall on them. The thought of their desertion is a cruel grief to Him; yet His words are full of tenderness and pity: "For it is written: I will strike the shepherd, and the sheep shall be dispersed." And then He goes on to console them with the assurance that, in spite of their unfaithfulness, they will still be dear to Him: "After I shall be risen again, I will go before you into Galilee."

* * *

"And Peter, answering, said to Him: Though all shall be scandalized in Thee, I will never be scandalized." Very pitiful is Peter's self-confidence. He had spoken in the same strain already, and Our Lord's solemn warning had passed unheeded. Now Jesus rebukes him once more: 'Amen, I say to thee, to-day, even this night, before the cock crow twice thou shalt deny Me thrice. Peter saith to Him: Though I should die with Thee, I will not deny Thee. And in like manner said all the disciples."

How often and how fervently have I declared my love for Thee, O Lord, only to fall away from Thee again!

* * *

"Then Jesus came with them to a country place which is called Gethsemani, and He said to His disciples: Sit you here till I go yonder and pray. And, taking with Him Peter and two sons of Zebedee"—the three who had seen His glory on Mount Thabor—'He began to grow sorrowful and to be sad."

He *began*. This is what St. Augustine would call "a watchful word"; for there is a deep significance in it. Our Saviour has always had every detail of His passion before His mind; yet it is only now that He begins to show His sorrow. As for me, no sooner have I anything to suffer than I either grow fretful or make a martyr of myself. Let me learn to bear my sorrows in silence. "Then He saith to them: My soul is sorrowful even unto death." "Stay you here and watch with Me." Saying these words, He staggers forward under that great load of heartrending sorrow, till He disappears from their sight in the little cavern where He was wont to pray.

So intense was His anguish that first a cold sweat broke out all over His body, standing in big drops upon His brow; then this sweat became tinged with blood, till at last it was pure blood that oozed from every pore, filling His garments and dropping from His face on to the ground.

* * *

Our Saviour prays: Father, if it be possible, let this chalice pass from Me" What an agony of woe breathes through this heartbroken petition! What fear, what sadness, what weariness! It teaches us that we, too, may pray for relief in sorrow; yet we must learn to add, as Jesus did: Nevertheless, not My will but Thine be done" His heart is perfectly submissive to the decree of His Father While as man He recoils from the appalling sacrifice demanded of Him, His Father's will is His will; nor does He for one moment set Himself in opposition to it

"And there appeared to Him an angel from heaven strengthening Him" Angels cannot suffer and therefore, though full of pity, cannot share in our sufferings; but Jesus is a real man and, like every son of Adam, feels the need of human sympathy So, while the angel returns to heaven, He goes to look for His three chosen friends He had told them to watch; He now finds them sleeping They have no sympathy to give Him; yet how gently He reproaches them! "Simon, sleepest thou? Couldst not thou watch with Me one hour? Watch and pray that ye enter not into temptation. The spirit indeed is willing; but the flesh is weak"

Love, we all know, is marvelously ingenious in finding excuses The two subjective conditions of sin are knowledge and consent, and Our Lord defends us on both counts It is the weakness of the flesh He pleads, not the unwillingness of the spirit. In His prayer for those who crucify Him, He excuses us for our want of full knowledge: "Father, forgive them for they know not what they do." Who can sound the depths of compassion in the heart of Christ?

Our Saviour then returned to His solitary prayer, and when after a while He came back to them "He found them again asleep, for their eyes were heavy; and they knew not what to answer Him."

Am I not in just the same case? I have

slept when I ought to have been watching; I have left my dear Lord to suffer alone, and I know not what to answer Him. All my grand protestations of love and loyalty have proved empty and worthless.

Christ has now entered into His eternal kingdom; yet He is still as human as ever. Has He not in these latter days come back to earth at Paray to complain that men love Him so little, to beg for their love? In the Holy Eucharist He is still longing for our sympathy.

"And He cometh the third time," His prayer being now finished, 'and saith to them: Sleep on now and take your rest. Behold, the hour is at hand, and the Son of Man shall be betrayed into the hands of sinners." There is a gentle irony in these sad words which must have touched them to the quick. It is too late now; they have missed their opportunity; the hour has come and they are not ready for it.

What bitterness there is for all of us in the thought of what might have been! If I had been more faithful, if I had but watched and prayed, how far otherwise I should have borne myself under temptation! how much remorse I should have been spared! how much suffering I should have spared my Saviour!

GETHSEMANI

GETHSEMANI

"Jesus, knowing that His hour was come that He should pass out of this world to the Father, having loved His own who were in the world, He loved them unto the end."
—*John xiii. 1.*

Supper over, He goes out with His disciples and crosses the brilliant city to the south gate, where a slope leads to the wooden bridge over the Brook Cedron. He follows the bridle-path on the east to a little square garden called Gethsemani, which means "Garden of olive-pressers."

Jerusalem, in the near distance, stands white and beautiful from out of a belt of woods. Opposite is the Gate Beautiful, and Olivet, is in front. As He passed the bridge over Cedron, He said to the eight: "Sit you here till I go yonder and pray." They are too sad at His words, and at the prospect of parting, to be able to pray. He takes on the three with Him. Think of that wonderful white-faced and white-robed figure when He says: "My soul is sorrowful even unto death." Never had He expressed His feelings so openly and utterly as now, and the three who once shared in the glory of the Transfiguration are now to share in His humiliation. Try to realize that, at the moment of which we are speaking, Our Saviour made a great act of contrition for the sins of the whole world, and that His Sacred Heart was nearly broken under the load. Clouds of sin rolled up upon Him until He was overwhelmed with their weight. Sin seems to have got the better of Him, and the blood of agony dropped from Him to the ground, staining the tender grass upon which the paschal moon was shedding its silvered light through the trees.

What a sight! "Is it nothing to you, all ye that pass by?" "Behold and see if there is any sorrow like unto My sorrow."

No wonder that the cry breaks from Him: "My Father, if it be possible, let this chalice pass from Me!" Yet, "Not as I will, but as Thou wilt."

So He prays, whilst He thinks of mankind, of you, and of me, bearing for us the weight of all our sins, hidden and forgotten, present, past, and to come. Sins of weakness, of malice, of pride, vanity, selfishness, innumerable.

He asks the Father to forgive them all, and bears the agony of their guilt. At last an angel comes to comfort Him and to give Him strength. He drinks the chalice and is ready to go forth and meet the enemy. Then they seize Him and drag Him to the courts. He is tied to a pillar and scourged before the people. A crown of thorns is pressed upon His brow, and at last He is stretched forth to be nailed to a cross, to be lifted up, and to die, in atonement for our sins. "Greater love than this hath no man, that a man lay down his life for his friends."

When you feel hard and dry and unable to make a good act of contrition, and when you fancy that your love has evaporated, just slip down on the ground before your crucifix and unite your sorrow with Our Lord's. Say that you are grieved for all you have done wrong, but that your trust is in Him. Say: O my Saviour, I grieve, with Thee for all my sins! Thy contrition has, I know, removed their guilt, and though I be red as scarlet, Thou wilt make me white as snow. I unite my contrition with Thine, both in life and in death."

If you are in sorrow and you feel sad and depressed, take your crucifix and the prayer of Christ will strengthen you. Strength is what we need and shall get through the agony in the Garden.

We are asked: "Can you drink of the chalice?" It is certain that Our Lord would rather send us sorrow than that we should have none. Sorrow is needed to soften our hearts, as fire softens wax. If your hearts are of wax they will soften; if of clay, sorrow will harden them, for fire softens wax but hardens clay. Our best friends are those who have been through sorrow. They are disciplined to Christ and are able to say: "Not my will, but Thine be done."

You can be useful to others in the measure in which you have suffered. You have to be tested.

—Vaughan' "Notes of Retreats."

"Blessed is the man whom God correcteth: refuse not therefore the chastising of the Lord."

—Job v. 17.

"We know that to them that love God all things work together unto good, to such as, according to His purpose, are called to be saints."

—Rom. viii. 28.

THE WILL OF GOD

The business to which we must apply ourselves in this world is to do the holy will of God in all things. The Son of God Himself had no other business during His mortal life than to do the will of His Father. He says expressly: "I came down from heaven not to do my own will, but the will of Him that sent Me" (John vi. 38). And again: "In the head of the book, it is written of Me, that I should do Thy will; O my God, I have desired it—in the midst of My heart" (Psalm xxxix). In this same Book of Life it is written also of all the children of God, that they likewise should do the will of their heavenly Father; this is the test by which we are all to be examined: all they that, with Jesus Christ, desire in the midst of their hearts, and like Him, embrace and love the holy will of God, and always conform themselves to it, shall be acknowledged for the true children of God and the brethren of Jesus Christ; but as many as shall revolt and fall off from their allegiance to the blessed will of God shall have their name blotted out of the Book of Life.

A perfect conformity with the will of God makes us even, as the Scripture says of David, "men according to God's own heart"; it is accompanied by perfect peace and tranquillity of mind in all events and circumstances, as being all ordered and directed by Him who is infinitely wise and infinitely good, and who appoints and ordains all things for the good of those who cast their whole care upon Him and who seek to please Him at all times.

"When we will what God wills," says St. Alphonsus, "it is our own greatest good that we will; for God desires what is for our greatest advantage. Let your constant practice be to offer yourself to God, that He may do with you what He pleases." God cannot be deceived, and we may rest assured that what He determines will be best for us. Can there be a better prayer than this: "Thy will be done?"

From all eternity God has been thinking of each one of us. Every flower we have ever looked upon, every inanimate or living thing, every sight and sound and taste that has ever given us innocent pleasure was designed from the beginning of creation for our sakes and meant to contribute to our happiness.

As to the everlasting happiness of heaven, we may well be content to leave our eternity in His keeping. He is the source of all that is good and desirable, and He has promised to give Himself to those that are faithful. "Fear not, Abram. I am thy protector, and thy reward exceeding great" (Gen. xv. 1).

WHAT MADNESS!

Man, being endowed with a will of his own, possesses the awful power of resisting the will of the Almighty; but this he does at his own great peril; for his true happiness both here and hereafter is bound up in submission to that will. Whenever he refuses to obey his conscience, he sets himself against God, for conscience is the voice of God. In this life he may defy His Maker; but not forever. The Almighty must prevail in the end.

What madness, then, to resist the irresistible! What madness to treat one's best friend as an enemy!

"Be you humbled, therefore, under the mighty hand of God, that He may exalt you in the time of visitation, casting all your care upon Him; for He hath care of you" (1 Pet. v. 6, 7).

Submission and confidence is my proper attitude, submission to God's power, confidence in God's kindness; for thus the divine omnipotence will be placed at my service. "He will do the will of them that fear Him" (Ps. cxliv. 19).

THE INFINITE WISDOM OF GOD

In all His dealings with man God shows Himself infinitely wise. He has given him intelligence to know his duty and free will to do it; and this free will He never takes away, however much it may be abused. He helps him with His grace to overcome the concupiscence of his corrupt nature and waits for him with unwearied patience, sending him afflictions, inded, but only to wean him from the dangerous love of this world, which attracts him as the flame attracts the moth; for the one object of this good Father is to save His child from casting himself into eternal misery and to secure his lasting happiness.

Yet, man will not trust himself to God's guidance. He thinks, poor fool, that he knows his own interests better and can take care of himself. He will put himself unreservedly in the hands of a physician and take cheerfully the remedies he prescribes, however unpleasant, for he holds bodily life and health to be worth any price; but of life and health eternal he reckons little.

For my part, I will leave myself in the care of the good God, Who knows infinitely better than I do what is profitable to me. It would be folly, indeed, not to trust One Who loves me so well.

LORD, I AM NOT WORTHY

TRUST IN GOD

Great indeed and very comforting are the promises made to prayer. *"Ask, and you shall receive.* It would seem from this that one has only to ask in the name of Christ and he is sure of getting what he wants; yet, common sense tells us that can not be the meaning intended. If it were, we Christians should ask for all the good things of life and get them, the hard and bitter things being left to those who had no faith; for, when any affliction threatened us, we should at once pray it away. It is evident, surely, that prayer is not meant to be simply an escape from suffering. Mark, now, that little clause: *"that your joy may be full";* for therein lies the explanation of Our Saviour's words. What joy is He thinking of? Eternal joy, of course. He binds Himself, therefore, to give us whatever will help us on our road to heaven. He will indeed hear and answer all our prayers; but if we make foolish petitions, He will answer them in His own wise and fatherly way by giving us something better. If we let our children have everything they cried for we should soon see them in their graves; and if God were to grant us everything we ask of Him, we should never rise to a better life.

GOD HATH CARE OF YOU

LET US ABANDON OURSELVES WHOLLY TO DIVINE PROVIDENCE!

There is perhaps no maxim which helps more than this to obtain the peace of heart and evenness of mind that belongs to a Christian life.

There is perhaps no maxim which, if this is practised with the simplicity and generosity of heart that it requires, renders the follower of Jesus Christ more dear to our heavenly Father. For, it implies perfect confidence in Him and in Him alone, complete detachment from all that appears delightful, powerful, and illustrious on earth, and a tender love, reserved for God alone. It implies a most lively faith, which believes as certain that all things in the world, both great and small, rest alike in the hand of our heavenly Father, and that nothing is done by them unless as disposed by Him for the accomplishment of His adorable designs. It implies also a belief in the infinite goodness, mercy, bounty, and generosity of our heavenly Father, who disposes all things for the good of them that trust in Him, and whose gifts and favors and care and graces are bestowed in proportion to the confidence of His well-beloved children.

The sure way by which the Christian may know if he is wanting in the full confidence that he is commanded to have in the provident care of his heavenly Father is to examine whether he feels any disquietude about the good and evil things of this world: whether he is always perfectly tranquil and calm, and prepared for whatever may happen; or is subject to anxiety, taking human measures with painful uneasiness as to their result, and, like a man of little faith, hoping and fearing excessively, and continually wavering.

—*Antonio Rosmini:*
Maxims of Christian Perfection.

* * *

Let the mercies of the Lord give glory to Him: and His wonderful works to the children of men.

They that go down to the sea in ships, doing business in the great waters:

These have seen the works of the Lord, and His wonders in the deep.

He said the word, and there arose a storm of wind: and the waves thereof were lifted up.

They mount up to the heavens, and they go down to the depths: their soul pined away with evils.

They were troubled, and reeled like a drunken man; and all their wisdom was swallowed up.

And they cried to the Lord in their affliction: and He brought them out of their distresses.

And He turned the storm into a breeze: and its waves were still.

And they rejoiced because they were still: and He brought them to the haven which they wished for.

Let the mercies of the Lord give glory to Him, and His wonderful works to the children of men.

—Ps. cvi. 21-31.

REQUIESCANT IN PACE

What is heavenly joy? The most concise definition of it we can look to find is contained in the Church's familiar prayer for her dead: "Eternal rest give to them, O Lord, and let perpetual light shine upon them. May they rest in peace. Amen." Eternal rest is the negative side of it, perpetual light the positive.

Of this latter St. Paul has written, quoting the prophet Isaias: "Eye hath not seen, nor ear heard, neither hath it entered into the heart of man, what things God hath prepared for them that love Him" (*1 Cor. ii. 9*).

Now, if heaven meant nothing more than eternal rest; that is, lasting and conscious deliverance from all the ills of this weary pilgrimage, would it not even then be worth all that we are called on to pay down for it? But it means so much more than this; and if even on this earth the good can for a little space so flood our soul with joy, if an enchanting scene or a strain of exquisite music, or the sense of love returned can so melt our hearts as to make us forgetful of all life's troubles, how will it be, think you, when the Lord of heaven and earth, the Source of all love and all beauty, lays Himself out to make His creatures happy? May we not be sure that He knows how to do it? Oh, in very truth: "Eye hath not seen, nor ear heard, neither hath it entered into the heart of man what things God hath prepared for them that love Him."

The souls of the just are in the hand of God, and the torment of death shall not touch them. In the sight of the unwise they seem to die, and their departure was taken for misery, and their going away from us, for utter destruction; but they are in peace, and though in the sight of men they suffered torments, their hope is full of immortality. Afflicted in few things, in many they shall be well rewarded; because God hath tried them, and found them worthy of Himself. As gold in the furnace He hath proved them, and as a victim of a holocaust He hath received them, and in time there shall be respect had to them. The just shall shine, and shall run to and fro like sparks among the reeds (*Wis. iii. 1-7*).

Then shall the just stand with great constancy against those that have afflicted them. . . . These, seeing it, shall be troubled with terrible fear, and shall be amazed at the suddenness of their unexpected salvation, saying within themselves, repenting and groaning for anguish of spirit:—These are they whom he had some time in derision, and for a parable of reproach. We fools esteemed their life madness, and their end without honor. Behold how they are numbered among the children of God, and their lot is among the saints (*Wis. v. 1-5*).

HEAVEN, OUR HOME

Naturally enough, the Thessalonians were anxious to learn from the apostle St. Paul what was the Christian teaching about the next world. Where were their beloved dead gone? The day returned after night, the spring followed winter, the cherry blossom and the apple bloom came back year by year, the skylark and the nightingale were heard when the snow was gone, and the olive and vine put forth their wealth of tender leaves, but alas! the long procession of their dear dead marched slowly to the tomb never to return. In their anxiety they turned to their Father in God. And he answers them in clear and definite words: "We will not have you ignorant, brethren, concerning them that are asleep, that you be not sorrowful, even as others who have no hope. For if we believe that Jesus Christ died and rose again, even so them who have slept in Jesus will God bring with Him. Wherefore comfort ye one another with these words."

Look up and realize that in the land very far off there is peace—a peace which comes from the harmony of order, life, and energy. See its symbol, not in the sluggish waters of a pool or a canal, but in the force of the ma-

Eye Hath Not Seen, Nor Ear Heard, What Things God Hath Prepared for Those That Love Him.

1 Cor. II, 9.

jestic river. See it, not in the pathless arid desert, or on the rocky height, but in the beautiful valley where flowers fill the air with sweetness and fruit is ripening. See it, not in the harp unstrung and put to rest, but in the energy and harmony of a perfect orchestra pouring forth a flood of glorious music.

Contemplate life with no shadow of death, health with no token of decay, strength with no sign of weakness, the eternal life, angelic, seraphic, godlike in a multitude of peace ever abiding

—*Bernard Vaughan, S.J.:*
Loaves and Fishes.

* * *

Foolish, indeed, are we, not to reflect oftener on the eternal home awaiting us, whose joys will never pall and whose transcendent bliss is everlasting.

When we find it hard to bear "the whips and scorns of time," let us encourage ourselves with the thought that the longest life is but brief, that no matter how storm-tossed our barque, we have but to keep courageously on our course, confident that He who launched our frail skiff on the seething waters, will guide it safely to the Eternal Shore, where, with gracious words of welcome on His dear lips, He will receive us into His

Father's Home. Then joy and rest shall be ours for evermore. God shall wipe away all tears from our eyes, and death shall be no more, nor mourning nor crying nor sorrow shall be any more, for the former things have passed away.

THE PROVIDENCE OF GOD

Not content with offering Himself to us as our last end, God, though respecting our free will, leads us by the hand to that blessed goal.

His providence has accompanied us through all the paths of life until this very moment.

Nothing in the world is abandoned to the caprice of chance.

Nothing is done except in the sight of God. Being infinite in His knowledge as in His other attributes, God sees everything.

"Neither is there any creature invisible in His sight: but all things are open to His eyes" (*Heb. iv. 13*).

This is a terrible thought for the sinner who offends Thee, O God, for Thou art the sure witness of the wickedness to which he abandons himself; but it is most consoling for the faithful soul whose trials Thou seest, whose sacrifices Thou reckonest, whose cries and prayers Thou hearest.

* * *

Nothing is done except by the permission of God.

To judge things superficially, it would seem that God is only an idle spectator of the events in the world. His hand is hidden. Except in some extraordinary circumstances,

His activity in the world is not apparent. The power of His creatures appears to possess unrestrained sovereignty. What makes the intervention of God in things here below even more difficult to perceive is that everything seems given over to the caprice of chance, to the sway of the passions, to the power of physical forces. In appearance, at least, confusion and disorder seem to rule.

Although hidden, the action of God is none the less real. While respecting the liberty of creatures, He rules it, directs its exercise, and limits it according to His own pleasure. The wicked themselves, to whom God has given such astonishing power for evil, accomplish only what He allows them to do. God, while seeming to leave a free field to human activity, confines it within limits which it will never exceed. Even when it goes astray and gives itself up to the greatest excesses, it is ever subordinated to the supreme will that governs it, against which it can do nothing; which says to it: "Thou shalt go no further" (*Job xxviii. 11*).

This empire of God over human wills appears most striking in relation to the Church, which wicked men can attack, persecute, even seem to conquer. But they can never succeed in destroying it. It is on this foundation that the Church places its unshaken confidence in the midst of strifes; and we know this confidence will not be confounded.

* * *

Nothing happens except in fulfillment of the providential plan of God. Since He is infinitely wise, God cannot do anything, cannot even admit anything useless or superfluous in His works. With how much greater reason must He exclude anything that would be an obstacle to the ends that He has prescribed. So, everything in the world has its end, its usefulness, a reason for its existence. Thus it is in the physical world, and it could not be otherwise in the moral world. Doubtless God does not will everything in the same way. He approves what is good; and, though tolerating evil, He forbids and condemns it. But since He admits both in His divine plan, He must have found the way to make them both serve the ends that He wills to attain and to make even sin contribute to the beauty and harmony of the universe.

As we well know, in the government of the world God has no other purpose but to sanctify His elect on earth that He may glorify them eternally in heaven. Such is the end that everything realizes after its own manner, and this is why the Apostle could say very truly that everything co-operates for the good of those who love God. "And we know that to them that love God all things work together unto good" (*Rom. viii. 23*).

Thus, my God, Thou showest that Thou art at once infinitely wise and infinitely good. Infinitely wise, since, without willing evil, Thou hast found the secret of making it serve in the accomplishment of Thy adorable designs; infinitely good, since the end to which Thou dost subordinate everything has been inspired by Thy love for us.

Such is the solid foundation of the peace and joy that sustains the faithful soul amid the strifes and trials that fill our life here below. It is convinced that God, Who directs all, will know how to turn even the saddest trial to its advantage, and that the thorns on the way will some day become jewels in its crown.

THE LOVING DISPENSATIONS OF DIVINE PROVIDENCE

Nothing happens in this world but by the direction or permission of God. "Nothing," says St. Augustine, "occurs by chance in the whole course of our life. God overrules all."

"Good things and evil, life and death, poverty and riches, are from God" (*Ecclus. xi. 14*). It may, perhaps be said that this holds good in sickness and in death, in cold and in heat, and in all the events of inanimate nature, but not in what depends upon the free will of man. You say, "if someone speaks evil of me, defrauds me, persecutes and ill-treats me, is that the will of God? How can I see God's will in that? Does He not forbid such actions? Consequently I can ascribe them only to the evil designs, to the wickedness or to the ignorance of men." But, I answer, God Himself speaks clearly and distinctly on this point. On His own Holy Word, we must believe that even what appears to be left to the caprice of men must be attributed to God's permission. The Jews imputed their captivity to other causes than the dispensation of Providence. The prophet Jeremias says: "Who is he that hath commanded a thing to be done, when the Lord commandeth it not? Shall not both evil and good proceed out of the mouth of the Most High?" (*Jeremias iii.* 37).

Therefore, when we are robbed of our good name, despoiled of our wealth, abused or otherwise wronged, we must ascribe it to the will of God. It is His hand that is visiting us; all is the work of His providence.

But, again, you object, 'All such actions are sinful. How can God will them? How can He take part therein? God's essence being holiness itself, He can have nothing in common with sin." I answer: In every evil deed two things must be clearly demonstrated; namely, the action itself, or the exterior movement; and the straying of the will from the Divine Law. Does your neighbor strike you, or calumniate you? You must, on the one hand, distinguish the motion of the arm or of the tongue; and, on the other, the evil intention that directs the movement. The movement itself is not sinful; therefore God can be the Author of it. And this He really is, for no creature has life or motion of itself; all receive it from God, who works in them and by them. The evil intention, on the contrary, is entirely the work of the human will, and it alone makes the sin. In this God takes no part. He permits the evil act in order not to do violence to the free will of men.

Accordingly, God shares in the deeds of men only insofar as He contributes to the exterior movement. The bad intention underlying the act proceeds from our will; and in this God has no part. You have abused your honor, your riches—God wills that you should lose the one or the other; but He takes no part in the sin of either the robber or the calumniator.

Patient endurance should characterize our conduct towards those to whom God has given command over us. We should neither judge their intentions nor harbor aversion against them. We should rest satisfied that, however hostile or inimical they may be toward us, they are only instruments of salvation in the hands of an All-good, All-wise, All-powerful God. He will give them no more power over us than is for our good. Creatures can do us no harm, unless power is given them from on high.

All enlightened souls have been firmly convinced of this truth. The history of Job presents a beautiful illustration of it. Job is bereft of his children and stripped of all his wealth; from the pinnacle of human happiness he falls to the depths of earthly misery, and what does he say? 'The Lord gave, the Lord hath taken away: as it hath pleased the

Lord, so is it done: blessed be the name of the Lord."

"Behold," says St. Augustine, "how this holy man understood the great mystery of God's providence! He did not say: 'The Lord hath given me children and riches, and the devil hath taken them from me.' But he said: 'The Lord hath given, the Lord hath taken. As it has pleased the Lord, and not as it has pleased the devil, also is it done.' Not less striking is the example of the Egyptian Joseph. His brothers, actuated by hatred and envy, sold him; but he ascribed all to God's providence. "God," he said, 'sent me before you into Egypt for your preservation, that you may be preserved upon the earth, and may have food to live. . . . Not by your counsel was I sent hither, but by the will of God" (*Gen. xiv, 5-8*).

Tobias, that faithful servant of God, was made blind while engaged in acts of charity. As we read in the Book of Tobias: 'This trial the Lord permitted to happen to him, that an example might be given to posterity of his patience, as also of holy Job. For whereas he had always feared God from his infancy, and kept his commandments, he repined not against God because the evil of blindness had befallen him. But continued immovable in the fear of God, giving thanks to God all the days of his life. For as the kings insulted over holy Job: so his relations and kinsmen mocked at his life, saying: Where is thy hope, for which thou gavest alms, and buriedst the dead? But Tobias rebuked them, saying: Speak not so: For we are the children of saints, and look for that life which God will give to those that never change their faith from Him."

David, pursued and insulted by Semei, sees the hand of Providence in the insolent behavior of his unruly subject. Twice did he restrain his indignant servant who wished to avenge him, with the words, "Let him alone and let him curse: for the Lord hath bid him curse David" *II Kings xvi. 10*). And Jesus Christ Himself, the Holy of Holies, Our Lord and Saviour, who came down from heaven to teach us by His word and example, did He not say to Peter, who with inconsiderate zeal urged Him to avert His sufferings and deliver Himself from the hands of His enemies: "The chalice which My Father hath given Me, shall I not drink it?" (*John xviii. 11*). Jesus attributed the ignominy and pain of His bitter torments, not to their immediate authors, not to the Jews that accused Him, not to Judas who betrayed Him, not to Pilate who condemned Him, not to the executioners who, with most horrible treatment, dragged Him to death, not to the devil, the instigator of the shocking deed: but only to God, in whom He saw, not a cruel Judge, but a loving Father.

We must not attribute our losses, our misfortunes, our sufferings, our humiliations, to the evil spirit or to man; but to their true author, God. Let us not venture to say: "This one or that one is the cause of my misfortune, my ruin." No, our trials are not the work of man. They are God's own work. This will redound to our greater tranquillity, for all that God, the best of fathers, does is full of infinite wisdom; all is subservient to His highest and holiest purposes.

ALONG THE ROYAL ROAD

God's providence rules and guides all things. He has not flung this world of ours into space to take its chance; but all nature, from the highest to the lowest forms in it, is under His constant control, everything that happens being ordered for the divine glory and the ultimate good of His Faithful servants. "We know that to them that love God all things work together unto good" (*Rom. viii. 28*). The sufferings of this life, no matter whence they come, bring home to us as nothing else can, the wretchedness of our fallen state, the gravity of sin, the worthlessness of earthly happiness, and so make us long for that better land "where the wicked cease from troubling and the weary are at rest" (*Job iii. 17*). Moreover, by accepting these afflictions in atonement for our sins, we can purify our souls and shorten our purgation hereafter.

Lastly, it is only along the Way of the Cross that we can tread in our Master's footsteps and find Him in eternal joy. "Through many tribulations we must enter into the kingdom of God" (*Acts xiv. 21*).

TRANQUILLITY

A holy Religious once remarked to his Superior in speaking of submission to the dispensations of dividine Providence:

"Success does not elate me, nor does misfortune cast me down; for, without losing time in examining, I take the one and the other equally from the hand of God. I do not desire things to turn out as I might naturally wish, but simply and only as God wills. All my prayers tend to one end; namely, that the will of God should be perfectly accomplished in me and in all creatures."

"But were you not disturbed," asked the Superior, "when an enemy set fire to our barn the other day, in consequence of which our entire harvest and all our cattle were destroyed?"

"No, Father," replied the Religious; "on the contrary, my custom is to thank God for such reverses, because I am firmly convinced that He permitted it only for His greater glory and our good. Therefore I did not concern myself as to whether much or little of our property escaped the flames; for I know that God, if we confide in Him, can feed us with a scrap of bread as well as with a whole barn full of grain. Hence, come what may, I am always peaceful and joyful."

The Superior admired his perfect conformity with the will of God, and his confidence in Divine Providence. He was no longer astonished at seeing this Religious working miracles.

We see by this example that conformity to God's will makes us not only holy, but also perfectly happy. It fills us with the sweetest peace that can be tasted in this life, and makes earth a paradise.

THE WEATHER

We should accept with tranquillity any kind of weather, heat and cold, rain and hail, storm and tempest. Why should a Christian lose his poise and serenity, when bad weather frustrates his plans or interferes with his pleasure?

Instead of becoming impatient and angry if the weather does not suit us, we should not only be satisfied with it, since God sent it; but even if it should particularly inconvenience us, we ought, with the three young men in the fiery furnace, exclaim: "Cold and heat, ice and snow, lightning and thunder, praise the Lord, praise and magnify Him forever." Inanimate nature honors the Lord unconsciously by fulfilling His holy will; we must glorify Him by acquiescing intelligently in all natural events. It often happens that that particular state of weather which proves so disagreeable to us is most acceptable to others. It thwarts our designs, but it may perhaps favor those of our fellow-men. And even if this were not so, do we not know that all kinds of weather contribute to the glory of God and the accomplishment of His holy will?

ST. FRANCIS DE SALES

The gentle Bishop of Geneva laid great stress at all times on the duty of bearing with our neighbor, and thus obeying the commandment of Holy Scripture: "Bear ye one another's burdens, and so you shall fulfill the law of Christ."

If today we put up with the ill-temper of our brother, tomorrow he will bear with our imperfections. We must in this life do like those who, walking on ice, give their hands to one another, so that if one slips, the other who has a firm foothold may support him.

St. John the Evangelist, towards the close of his life, exhorted his brethren not to deny one another this support, but to foster mutual charity, which prompts the Christian to help his neighbor, and is one of the chiefest precepts of Jesus Christ, Who, true Lamb of God, endured, and carried on His shoulders, and on the wood of the cross, all our sins—an infinitely heavy burden, nor to be borne by any but Him. The value set by our blessed Father on this mutual support was marvelous, and he went so far as to look upon it as the crown of our perfection.

He says on the subject to one who was very dear to him: "It is a great part of our perfection to bear with one another in our imperfections; for there is no better way of showing our own love for our neighbor.'

God will, in His mercy, bear with him who has mercifully borne with the defects of his neighbor.

St. Francis de Sales made himself *all things to all men*. His characteristic virtues were unflagging zeal in union with unruffled gentleness. He maintained perfect calmness in the midst of the greatest tribulations.

TRIBULATIONS

Tribulations are an essential feature in the means that work unto salvation. "For gold and silver are tried in the fire, but acceptable men in the furnace of humiliation" (*Ecclus. ii. 5*). Temptations are necessary. In refusing to accept them, we become our own enemies. We are in the hands of God like a block of marble in the hands of the sculptor. To form a beautiful statue, the workman must use the chisel and the hammer; he must hew and hack the marble; he must make the splinters fly. God intends to fashion us to His own image; therefore, we must passively submit to His skilful hand. Every stroke is a master-touch toward our sanctification. "For this is the will of God, your sanctification," says St. Paul. Yes, our sanctification is the only end God has in view in all that He sends us.

Perfection consists in nothing else than in conformity to the will of God. The more fully we submit to the Divine Will the more we advance; when he resist it, we go backward. St. Teresa said to her spiritual daughters: 'Direct your prayer to one thing only; that is, to conform your will perfectly to the Divine Will. Be assured that there is no greater perfection attainable than this conformity, and that they who most earnestly strive for it will receive from God the richest graces and most quickly advance in the interior life. Believe me, this is the secret. Upon this point alone rests our sanctification."

The submission of our will is the most pleasing sacrifice that we can make to God, and the one that honors Him most. It is the most perfect act of love, the most elevating and meritorious virtue. By it we can at every moment amass incomparable treasures of grace, and gain in a short time the richest merits for eternity.

THE PATH OF PERFECTION

In order to keep ourselves in the path of perfection, swerving neither to the right nor the left, the soul must follow no inspiration which she assumes comes from God without first assuring herself that it does not interfere with the duties of her state in life. These duties are the most certain indications of the will of God, and nothing should be preferred to them; in fulfilling them there is nothing to be feared, no exclusion or discrimination to be made; the moments devoted to them are the most precious and salutary for the soul from the fact that she is sure of accomplishing the good pleasure of God. All the perfection of the saints consists in their fidelity to the order of God; therefore we must refuse nothing, seek nothing, but accept all from His hand, and nothing without Him. Books, wise counsels, vocal prayers, interior affections, if they come to us in the order of God, instruct, guide and unite the soul to Him. Quietism errs when it disclaims these means and all sensible appearances, for there are souls whom God wills shall be always led in this way, and their state and their attractions clearly indicate it. In vain we picture to ourselves methods of abandonment whence all action is excluded. When the order of God causes us to act, our sanctification lies in action.

I Am the Way

Besides the duties of each one's state, God may further ask certain actions which are not included in these duties, though not contrary to them. Attraction and inspiration, then indicate the divine order; and the most perfect for souls whom God leads in this way is to add to things of precept, things inspired, but always with the precautions which inspiration requires to prevent its interfering with the duties of one's state and the ordinary events of Providence.

God makes saints as He chooses. They are formed by His divine action, to which they are ever submissive, and this submission is the truest abandonment and the most perfect.

Fidelity to the duties of one's state and submission to the dispositions of Providence are common to all the saints. They live hidden in obscurity, for the world is so fatal to holiness that they would avoid its quicksands; but not in this does their sanctity consist, but wholly in their entire submission to the order of God. The more absolute their submission, the greater their sanctity. We must not imagine that those whose virtues God is pleased to brilliantly manifest by singular and extraordinary works, by undoubted attractions and inspirations, are any less faithful in the path of abandonment. Once the order of God makes these brilliant works a duty, they fail in abandonment to Him and His will, which ceases to rule their every moment, and their every moment ceases to be the exponent of the will of God if they content themselves with the duties of their state and the ordinary events of Providence. They must study and measure their efforts according to the standard of God's designs for them in that path which their attractions indicate to them. Fidelity to inspiration is for them a duty; and as there are souls whose duty is marked by an exterior law, and who must be guided by it because God confines them to it, so also there are others who, besides their exterior duties, must be further faithful to that interior law which the Holy Spirit engraves upon their hearts.

But who are the most perfect? Vain and idle research! Each one must follow the path which is traced for him. Perfection consists in absolute submission to the order of God and carefully availing ourselves of all that is most perfect therein. It advances us little to weigh the advantages of the different states considered in themselves, since it is neither in the quality nor quantity of things enjoined that sanctity is to be sought. If self-love be the principle of our actions, or if we do not correct it when we recognize its workings, we shall be always poor in the midst of an abundance not provided by the order of God. However, to decide in a measure the question, I think that sanctity corresponds to the love one has for God's good pleasure; and the greater one's love for this holy will and this order, whatever the character of their manifestations, the greater one's sanctity. This is manifest in Jesus, Mary and Joseph, for in their private life there is more of love than of grandeur, and more of spirit than of matter; and it is not written that these sacred persons sought the holiest of things, but holiness in all things.

We must therefore conclude that there is no special way which can be called the most perfect, but that the most perfect in general is fidelity to the order of God, whether in the accomplishment of exterior duties or in the interior dispositions, each one according to his state and calling.

I believe that if souls seriously aspiring to perfection understood this, and knew how direct is their path, they would be spared much difficulty. I say the same equally of souls living in the world and of souls consecrated to God. If the first knew the means of merit afforded them by their ever-recurring daily duties and the ordinary actions of their state in life; if the second could persuade themselves that the foundation of sanctity lies in those very things which they consider unimportant and even foreign to them; if both could understand that the crosses sent by Providence which they constantly find in their state in life lead them to the highest perfection by a surer and shorter path than do extraordinary states or extraordinary works; and that the true philosopher's stone is submission to the order of God, which changes into pure gold all their occupations, all their weariness, all their sufferings—how happy they would be! What consolation and what courage they would gather from this thought, that to acquire the friendship of God and all the glory of heaven they have but to do what they are doing, suffer what they are suffering; and that what they lose and count as naught would not suffice to obtain them eminent sanctity. O my God, that I might be the missionary of Thy holy will, and teach the whole world that there is nothing so easy, so simple, so within the reach of all, as sanctity! Would that I could make them understand that, just as the good and the bad thief had the same to do and suffer to obtain their salvation, so two souls, one worldly and the other wholly interior and spiritual, have nothing more to do, one than the other; that she who sanctifies herself acquires eternal happiness by doing in submission to the will of God what she who is lost does through caprice; and that the latter is lost by suffering unwillingly and impatiently what she who is saved endures with resignation. The difference, therefore, is only the heart.

O dear souls, let me repeat to you: Sanctity will cost you no more; do what you are doing; suffer what you are suffering: it is only your heart that need be changed. By the heart we mean the will. This change, then, consists in willing what comes to us by the order of God. Yes, holiness of heart is a simple *fiat,* a simple disposition of conformity to the will of God. And what is easier? For who could not love so adorable and merciful a will? Let us love it, then, and through this love alone all within us will become divine.

AN ACT OF ABANDONMENT

By Blessed Joseph Pignatelli, S. J.

O my God, I know not what must come to me to-day; but I am certain that nothing can happen to me which Thou hast not foreseen and ordained from all eternity: that is sufficient for me. I adore Thy impenetrable and eternal designs, to which I submit with all my heart; I desire, I accept them all, and I unite my sacrifice to that of Jesus Christ, my divine Saviour; I ask in His name, and through His infinite merits, patience in my trials, and perfect submission to all that comes to me by Thy good pleasure. Amen.

AN ACT OF CONFIDENCE IN GOD

By Blessed Claude De La Colombiere, S.J.

My God, I believe so firmly that Thou watchest over all who hope in Thee, and that we can want for nothing when we rely upon Thee in all things, that I am resolved for the future to have no anxieties, and to cast all my cares upon Thee. *"In peace in the self-same I will sleep and I will rest; for Thou, O Lord, singularly hast settled me in hope."*

Men may deprive me of worldly goods and of honors; sickness may take from me my strength and the means of serving Thee; I may even lose Thy grace by sin: but my trust shall never leave me; I will preserve it to the last moment of my life, and the powers of hell shall seek in vain to wrest it from me. *"In peace in the self-same I will sleep and I will rest."*

Let others seek happiness in their wealth, in their talents; let them trust to the purity of their lives, the severity of their mortifications, to the number of their good works, the fervor of their prayers; as for me, O my God, in my very confidence lies all my hope. *"For Thou, O Lord, singularly hast settled me in hope."* This confidence can never be in vain. *"No one has hoped in the Lord has been confounded."*

I am assured, therefore, of my eternal happiness, for I firmly hope for it, and all my hope is in Thee. *"In Thee, O Lord, have I hoped; let me never be confounded."*

I know, alas! I know but too well that I am weak and unstable; I know the power of temptation against the strongest virtue. I have seen stars fall from heaven, and pillars of the firmament totter; but these things alarm me not. While I hope in Thee, I am sheltered from all misfortune, and I am sure that my trust shall endure, for I rely upon Thee to sustain this unfailing hope. Finally, I know that my confidence cannot exceed Thy bounty, and that I shall never receive less than I have hoped for from Thee. Therefore I hope that Thou wilt sustain me against my evil inclinations; that Thou wilt protect me against the most furious assaults of the evil one, and that Thou wilt cause my weakness to triumph over my most powerful enemies. I hope that Thou wilt never cease to love me, and that I shall love Thee unceasingly.

BLESSED ARE THE PEACEMAKERS

Reflect upon the words of the seventh Beatitude: 'Blessed are the peacemakers, for they shall be called the children of God."

God's own abode is in eternal peace, and the heavenly Jerusalem is the vision and enjoyment of an undisturbed, everlasting peace.

They therefore that truly love peace, and as much as lies in them both keep it in themselves and with all others, and contribute all they can to make peace among such as are at variance with one another and to bring all their neighbors to be at peace with God are entitled to this beatitude, and to the glorious character of children of God. Oh, how amiable is this spirit of peace! How blessed are its fruits! It is the paradise of the soul: it makes a kind of a heaven upon earth. May this 'peace of God which surpasseth all understanding, keep both our heart and minds in Christ Jesus our Lord!" (Philip. iv. 7).

Consider the different ways there are of being peacemakers, with relation to our neighbors, with relation to ourselves, and with relation to God. 'Tis a blessed thing to bring our neighbors to peace and mutual charity; as "it is an abomination in the sight of God to sow discord among brethren" (Prov. vi. 19).

BLESSED ARE THE PEACEMAKERS

'Tis a more blessed thing to make peace at home in our own souls by suppressing the rebellious disorders of our passions, by bringing the flesh under subjection to the spirit, the inferior part of the soul to the superior, and the superior to God. 'Tis the most blessed thing of all to bring both ourselves and as many others as we can to a constant and perfect peace with God, that He may reign without control in all our souls; that His kingdom may be perfectly established within us; that His holy will, His holy law, His grace, and His peace may live in us and with us forever. O happy peace indeed, that unites us here to God by grace, and hereafter in eternal glory!

Consider, moreover, the reward promised in this Beatitude to the peacemakers: "they shall be called the children of God." Reflect, my soul, what a dignity it is to be the children of so great a King, even the King that made heaven and earth. "Behold, what manner of charity," said St. John (1 John iii. 1), "the Father hath bestowed upon us, that we should be called and should be the sons of God." Sons of God, even now by His grace, bearing a resemblance with His true Son (who is styled in Scripture the *Prince of Peace*) and as such in a particular manner loved, cherished, and protected by Him here as a parent;

and hereafter to be admitted to a more perfect likeness, union, and, as it were, transformation into Him, according to the words of the same Apostle (v. 2): "Dearly beloved, we are now the sons of God, and it hath not yet appeared what we shall be. We know that when He shall appear, we shall be like unto Him; because we shall see Him as He is." O Christians, what blessings both for time and for eternity are prepared for the lovers and promoters of peace!

PEACE IN ABSOLUTE SURRENDER TO DIVINE PROVIDENCE *

Two principles form the unalterable basis of the virtue of abandonment.

First principle: Nothing is done, nothing happens, either in the material or in the moral world, which God has not foreseen from all eternity, and which He has not willed, or at least permitted.

Second principle: God can will nothing, He can permit nothing, but in view of the end He proposed to Himself in creating the world; i.e., in view of His glory and the glory of the Man-God, Jesus Christ, His only Son.

To these two principles we shall add a third, which will complete the elucidation of this whole subject: As long as man lives upon earth, God desires to be glorified through the happiness of this privileged creature; and consequently in God's designs the interest of man's sanctification and happiness is inseparable from the interest of the divine glory.

If we do not lose sight of these principles, which no Christian can question, we shall understand that our confidence in the Providence of our Father in heaven cannot be too

---

* From Fr. De Caussade's *Abandonment*, Revised by Rev. H. Ramière, S.J.

great, too absolute, too child-like. If nothing but what He permits happens, and if He can permit nothing but what is for our happiness, then we have nothing to fear, except not being sufficiently submissive to God. As long as we keep ourselves united with Him and we walk after His designs, were all creatures to turn against us they could not harm us. He who relies upon God becomes by this very reliance as powerful and as invincible as God, and created powers can no more prevail against him than against God Himself.

This confidence in the fatherly providence of God cannot, evidently, dispense us from doing all that is in our power to accomplish His designs; but after having done all that depends upon our efforts, we will abandon ourselves completely to God for the rest.

This abandonment should extend, in fact, to everything—to the past, to the present, to the future; to the body and all its conditions; to the soul and all its miseries, as well as all its qualities; to blessings; to afflictions; to the good will of men, and to their malice; to the vicissitudes of the material, and the revolutions of the moral, world; to life and to death. However, as these different orders of things do not enter in the same manner in the designs of divine Providence, neither should our abandonment in regard to these be practised in the same manner; and the rules which we should follow in the practice of this virtue should be founded on the nature itself of the objects which call it forth. We shall indicate the principal ones.

I. Among all the dispositions to which our abandonment can be applied, there are, first, those which depend solely upon God, where human liberty has no part either in producing or averting them. Such are, for example, certain scourges, and vicissitudes of the atmosphere; certain accidents impossible to foresee, certain natural defects of body or soul.

In regard to facts of this order, whether of the past, present or future, it is evident that our abandonment cannot be too absolute.

There is nothing to do here but to passively and lovingly endure all that God sends us; to blindly accept in advance all that it may please Him to send us in the future. Resistance would be useless, and only serve to make us unhappy; a loving and frequently renewed acceptance, on the contrary, would make these inevitable sufferings very meritorious.

II. There are other sufferings which come to us through the malice of creatures: persecutions, calumnies, ill-treatment, neglect, injustice and offences of every kind. What are we to do when we find ourselves exposed to vexatious things of this sort?

1. We evidently cannot like the offense against God with which they are accompanied; we should, on the contrary, deplore and detest it, not because it wounds our self-love, but because it is an offense against the divine rights, and compromises the salvation of the offending souls.

2. As for that which concerns us, on the contrary, we should regard as a blessing that which is in itself an evil; and to do this we need only recall the principles previously laid down: not to look only at the creature who is the immediate cause of our sufferings, but to raise our eyes higher and behold God, who has foreseen and permitted them from all eternity, and who in permitting them had only our happiness in view. This thought will be sufficient to dissipate the bitterness and trouble which would take possesion of our hearts were we to look only at the injustice of which we are the victims.

3. In regard to the effects of this injustice already consummated and irreparable, we have only to resign ourselves as lovingly as possible, and carefully gather their precious fruits. It is frequently not difficult to divine

the spiritual fruits God destined for us in exposing us to temporal evils: to detach us from creatures; to deliver us from inordinate affections, from our pride, from our tepidity—veritable maladies of the soul, frequently all the more dangerous as they are less perceptible, and of which the heavenly Physician wishes to cure us, using the malice of our neighbor as a sharp instrument. We do not hesitate to endure much greater sufferings to be delivered from corporal infirmities; then let us gratefully accept the spiritual health, infinitely more precious, which God offers us, however disagreeable the instrument through which He gives it to us.

4. If it is in our power to avert the consequences of malice and injustice, and if in our true interest, and in the interest of the divine glory, we deem it necessary to take any measures to this end, let us do so without departing from the practice of the holy virtue of abandonment. Let us commit the success of our efforts to God, and be ready to accept failure if God judges it more suitable to His designs and more profitable to our souls. We are so blind that we always have reason to fear being deceived; but God cannot be deceived, and we may be certain, in advance, that what He determines will be best. There-

fore we cannot do better than abandon with fullest confidence the result of our efforts to Him.

III. But should this abandonment extend equally to our acts of imprudence, to our faults, and all the annoyances of every kind in which they may result?

It is important to distinguish here two things which self-love tends to confound. In the fault itself we must distinguish what is culpable and what is humiliating. Likewise in its consequences we must distinguish what is detrimental to the divine glory and the confusion inflicted on our self-love. Evidently we cannot hate too much the fault, properly so called, nor regret too keenly the injury done to the divine glory. But as for our humiliation, and the confusion inflicted on our self-love, we should rejoice, and acquiesce in it with complete abandonment. This kind of sacrifice is undoubtedly the best fitted to destroy in us the most secret fibres of self-love, and to cause us to make rapid progress in virtue. To souls who have attained a certain degree of regularity and detachment, exterior humiliations are very little. When we have learned the vanity of human glory, we easily endure the sting of contempt; but we may still unite with this exterior detachment great attachment to our own esteem and approbation, and a wholly egotistical desire of perfection. In this case, self-love, by changing its object, would only become more dangerous. To destroy it, there is no remedy more efficacious than the humiliation resulting from our faults; and we cannot, consequently, strive too earnestly to apply the practice of abandonment to this humiliation, endeavoring at the same time to correct the faults themselves.

And what we say of faults of the past applies equally to faults of the future. The practice of abandonment well understood should deliver us from that impatience which makes us wish to at once attain the summit of perfection, and which only serves to keep us from it by turning us from the only path which leads to perfection. This path is humility, and the impatience which we are censuring is only another form of pride. Let us make every effort to correct our faults; but let us be resigned to not seeing them all disappear in a day. Let us earnestly, and with the most filial confidence, ask God to grant us that decisive grace which will completely wrest us from ourselves, to make us live only in Him; but let us leave to Him, with an equally filial abandonment, the care of determining the day and hour in which this grace shall be given us.

With still greater reason should we abandon to God the determining of the degree of sanctity which we shall attain upon earth, the extraordinary graces which will accompany this sanctity here below, and the glory with which it will be crowned in heaven. In so far as it depends upon us, we should leave nothing undone to increase this sanctity and this glory, in order not to fall short of the degree God has marked for us; but if we must earnestly devote ourselves to realizing His designs, we must not desire to have them other than they are. If our love for God is what it should be, we will thank Him for having granted other souls favors that He has refused us, and we will praise Him no less for our poverty than for our riches.

* * *

We all know that sanctification is a work both divine and human. It is divine through its immediate principle, the Holy Spirit; through its meritorious cause, the Incarnation and the death of the Son of God; through its end, the happiness of the Holy Trinity, in which holy souls are to participate for all eternity; finally, through its chief means, the teachings and the graces of Jesus Christ transmitted to men through the Church.

But this work is human also, since the graces of the Holy Spirit, the merits of the Son of God, the designs of the Holy Trinity, and all the efforts of Providence can bear fruit in a soul only so far as she freely co-operates with them.

This co-operation in our sanctification which God requires of us is composed of three parts.

It consists, first of all, in the destruction of everything in our corrupt nature which is an obstacle to the divine action: sins, vices, sensible inclinations, defects, imperfections. This first labor is what the masters of the spiritual life call the *purgative way*. It is accomplished by examination of conscience, works of penance and mortification, and the various practices in use in the Church.

The second part of the labor which God imposes on the soul desirous to attain sanctity is less painful, and easier. It is what is called the *illuminative way*. The soul that God introduces therein exercises herself in producing the interior acts of virtue with which grace inspires her, and in practising the good works to which this same grace impels her.

Finally, when the obstacles are removed

and the soul's preparation is completed, God unites Himself to her, fills her with His grace, inflames her with His love, and uses her as a docile instrument for the accomplishment of His designs: this is the *unitive way*.

But let us not misapprehend this condition. Even in this perfect state in which God is fully master of His reasonable creature, He does not act in her without her co-operation; He requires of her great fidelity in avoiding the smallest faults, great vigilance over her affections, great generosity in denying herself in all things, great fervor in prayer. So far from dispensing her from the works of the illuminative way by which she prepared herself for the divine union, He causes her to accomplish them with greater perfection and merit.

Among these works common to the two ways of which we have just spoken, there are some which are strictly of obligation, either because they are prescribed to all Christians by the commandments of God and the Church, or because they are imposed on each one by the special circumstances of his state. There are others which are simply of counsel, or even purely of supererogation, and which each one embraces according to the greater or less ardor of his desire for sanctity. In the same way, among the works of penance which form the purgative way there are some from which no one can dispense himself; but there are others which, without being of absolute necessity, are more or less useful, or even relatively necessary to certain souls because of their particular position, and the violence of the inclinations which impel them to evil.

Such is man's threefold part in the beginning, progress and consummation of the eminently divine work of sanctification—a part essentially active, and so necessary that without it God's part would be hopelessly sterile.

But if God does not dispense Christians from laboring actively for their salvation, He takes upon Himself the greatest part of this work; He unceasingly labors thereon; He employs all creatures and all events to further it; and if they will only permit Him to do His will—without doing any more than they are doing, without suffering, but only by recognizing and loving God's action in things which He obliges them to do and suffer, they will amass priceless merits and attain great perfection.

INDULGENCED EJACULATION OF RESIGNATION TO THE WILL OF GOD

Fiat, laudetur, atque in æternum superexaltetur justissima, altissima, et amabilissima voluntas *Dei* in omnibus.	May the most just, most high, and most adorable will of *God* be in all things done, praised, and magnified for ever.

i. Indulgence 100 days, once a day.
ii. Plenary, *in articulo mortis* (at the point of death), to those who, during life, shall have frequently recited this Ejaculation, provided that, worthily disposed, they accept death with resignation from the hands of God.
—*The Raccolta.*

A PLENARY INDULGENCE AT THE HOUR OF DEATH

By a decree of the Sacred Congregation of Indulgences of March 9, 1904, Pope Pius X granted a plenary indulgence at the moment of death to all the faithful who, on any day they may choose, shall receive the sacraments of Penance and Holy Eucharist and make the following act with sincere love toward God.

O Lord my God, I now at this moment readily and willingly accept at Thy hand whatever kind of death it may please Thee to send me, with all its pains, penalties, and sorrows.

PRAYER FOR PERSEVERANCE

O Lord Almighty, Who permittest evil to draw good therefrom, hear our humble prayers, and grant that we remain faithful to Thee unto death. Grant us also, through the intercession of most holy Mary, the strength ever to conform ourselves to Thy most holy will.

Indulgence: 100 days, once a day.—Pius IX, June 15, 1862; Leo XIII, July 19, 1890.

May the God of peace, who brought again from the dead the great Pastor of the sheep, our Lord Jesus Christ, in the blood of the everlasting testament, fit you in all goodness, that you may do His will; doing in you that which is well pleasing in His sight, through Jesus Christ, to whom is glory forever and ever. Amen.

—Heb. xii, 20-21.

PEACE OF MIND

Learn to listen with a patient and willing mind to those who point out to thee thy faults, esteeming their judgment to be more correct when they reprove thee than thy own when thou excusest thyself. Oh, that thou wert no more moved by just praises or unjust reproofs than if they were not spoken of thyself! thou wouldst ascribe the first to God, and impute the last to thyself, committing them to God.

If thou hast rested thy peace of mind on the words of men, and not on the testimony of thy conscience and on thy God, thou wilt easily lose it, and be troubled. Let men hear what opinion they will of thee; let it be enough for thee that thou art pleasing to Him Who *is the searcher of hearts and veins* (Ps. vii. 10). Nevertheless, after the example of the apostle St. Paul, provide *good things not only in the sight of God, but also in the sight of all men* (Rom. xii. 17).

ADVERSITIES

Receive all adverse things lovingly, as most precious gifts sent to thee from God. Think

"REFUSE NOT, THEREFORE THE CHASTISING OF THE LORD"
Job. 5, 17

not that anything happens to thee except by the dispensation of Divine Providence; for, unless the Lord permitted it, thou wouldst suffer no adversity.

When our common enemy inflicted on the blessed Job the loss of his goods and of his children, the holy man said not, the Lord gave, and the devil hath taken away; but what saith he? 'The Lord gave, and the Lord hath taken away; as it hath pleased the Lord, so is it done: blessed be the name of the Lord" (Job. i. 21).

Be not angry with men who injure thee; but, recognizing in them the instrument of the divine dispensations, love them, and give thanks to God. Regard with the eyes of thy heart Him Who allows thee to be tried by troubles, rather than those who trouble thee.

Although God may purge, purify, and prove thee, He does not forsake thee. For 'the Lord is nigh unto them that are of a contrite heart, and He will save the humble of spirit" (Ps. xxxiii, 19). Perhaps thou knowest not now why He thus bruises and chastises thee; but, when thou art come to Him, thou wilt recognize that those scourges with which He now tries thee, came only from His love of thee. He permits no misfortune, however trifling, to happen without its being for the exceeding advantage of him who suffers it, if he is patient. The humble endurance of interior dereliction is more pleasing to Him than great sweetness of devotion. He will not suffer thee to be tempted beyond thy strength, provided thou trustest not in thyself, but in Him; provided thou art patient, and waitest in holy confidence for His help.

REMAIN TRANQUIL

He labors under a dangerous disease who willingly speaks of the vices of others, and discloses them rashly. Such a one often covers with a false pretext of zeal for piety and justice the things which he says out of mere levity or from a bad disposition.

When thou hast to reprove any one, exhort and admonish him rather than reproach or revile him, so long as the matter admits of gentleness. If severity is necessary, see that thou art severe without bitterness. Let not anger or any selfish motive urge thee to more vehement correction, but only the love of God and the good of souls. Let thy reason remain ever tranquil. Let holy discretion rule and temper even the severity of thy words. Persecute the sin, not the man. For man is a good thing, created by God; sin is a bad thing, made by man. When thou seemest outwardly to inveigh sharply against anyone, inwardly pity him with secret affection, and in thy heart prefer him to thyself. If thou feelest thy mind to be seriously disturbed, either defer the correction till the disturbance has passed away, or speak but a few words without impetuosity.

—*Ludovicus Blosius:*
The Paradise of the Faithful Soul.

PEACE OF SOUL AFTER A FAULT

God does not say to the Prodigal: 'After some time, if I see that you really do keep your resolutions, I may reinstate you in My favor." No; the very first moment that he has humbly acknowledged his sin, God receives him with joy, and cannot do enough to honor him, and make him feel at home.

When a person of mere ordinary virtue commits a sin, it takes him some time to feel the same toward God as he did before. He cannot realize the wonderful generosity of the heart of God. When a saint commits a sin, he runs to God at once like a little child to its mother, and confesses it humbly, without excuse or palliation, like a brave, honest, confiding child. Then the next moment he is just as happy with God as he was before. The fault makes no more difference to him. The saint understands sin better than the ordinary person, but what is far more important, he understands God better.

One of the great signs of progress in the spiritual life is this quick return and peace of soul after a fault.

LIBERTY OF SPIRIT

Distractions and tediousness in prayer do not matter at all so long as your heart is with

Our Lord. You must humble yourself as much as you can. God loves humble souls and gives His graces to them.

Do not worry yourself about recalling the thought of the presence of God at special times. He lives in your heart: keep a calm liberty of spirit. Don't be narrow or straitlaced in any way.

* * *

God does not want our spiritual life to be a constant stress, uneasy, foggy, stormy. He loves peace and joy and spiritual gayety. We often offend other people without meaning to do so. But God knows us through and through and understands what we mean. We never offend Him unless we *want* to offend Him.

PRAY IN THE WAY THAT YOU LIKE BEST

Bearing in union with His passion the little humiliations, rebuffs, and trials of everyday life brings us wonderfully near to Our Lord and to sanctity.

The spiritual life is the easiest, sweetest and happiest thing in the world—to love God and be loved by Him.

To do His will is to love Him.

His will is to be found in the ordinary little things of every minute.

We please Him and win His love in the same way as we please and win an earthly friend.

There are very few invariable rules in the spiritual life, but this is one: Pray in the way that you like best.

—*Father Considine, S.J.*

MY PEACE I GIVE UNTO YOU

Solomon, having prayed for wisdom, received every other good thing along with it; and we too, if, like good Christians, we leave ourselves in our heavenly Father's hands and have no other wish but to please Him, shall most certainly have many temporal blessings poured out upon us. God will never send us a life wholly free from suffering, for that is not the way to heaven; but He will give us peace, that peace which surpasseth all understanding, leading through storm and sunshine to eternal joy. 'Peace I leave with you. My peace I give unto you; not as the world giveth do I give unto you" (John xiv. 27).

* * *

Strive to banish from your own interior whatsoever may disturb the tranquillity of your soul. Adopt the *Book-Mark of Saint Teresa:*

> Let nothing disturb thee,
> Nothing affright thee;
> All things are passing;
> God never changeth;
> Patient endurance
> Attaineth to all things;
> Who God possesseth
> In nothing is wanting;
> Alone God sufficeth.

This inward peace, when it is perfect is a certain foretaste of heaven; it is a kind of heaven upon earth. In such souls God is pleased to dwell, of whom the Royal prophet sings (Ps. lxxv), that 'His place is in peace, and his abode in Sion." To come at this happy peace (besides taking care to keep peace with God, by a clean conscience, and with every neighbor, by concord and charity) we must have our passions mortified, our affections well ordered and regulated, and our desires restrained; we must banish all hurry and over-eagerness; all sadness and melancholy; all scrupulous fears, anxious cares, and uneasiness about the things of this world; and, above all things, and in all things, we must conform ourselves to the holy will of God. Practise these lessons, my soul, and thou wilt be at peace, at least as far as the condition of thy mortal pilgrimage will allow.

Whatsoever shall befall the just man, it shall not make him sad.

—Prov. xii. 21.

*　*　*

Take all that shall be brought upon thee, and in thy sorrow endure, and in thy humiliation keep patience.

—Ecclus. ii. 4.

I reckon that the suffering of this time are not worthy to be compared with the glory to come, that shall be revealed in us.

* * *

And we know that to them that love God, all things work together unto good, to such as, according to His purpose, are called to be saints.
—*St. Paul to the Romans: viii, 18, 28.*

* * *

Sweet are the uses of adversity,
Which like the toad, ugly and venomous,
Wears yet a precious jewel in his head;
And this our life, exempt from public haunt,
Finds tongues in trees, books in the running brooks,
Sermons in stones, and good in everything.
—*Shakespeare: As You Like It.*

THE PEACE OF GOD

We ask for Peace, O Lord!
  Yet not to stand secure,
Girt round with iron Pride,
  Contented to endure:
Crushing the gentle strings
  That human hearts should know,
Untouched by others' joy
    Or others' woe;—
Thou, O dear Lord, wilt never teach us so.

We ask Thy Peace, O Lord!
  Through storm, and fear, and strife,
To light and guide us on,
  Through a long, struggling life:
While no success or gain
  Shall cheer the desperate fight,
Or nerve, what the world calls,
    Our wasted might:—
Yet pressing through the darkness to the light.

It is Thine own, O Lord,
  Who toil while others sleep;
Who sow with loving care
  What other hands shall reap:
They lean on Thee entranced,
  In calm and perfect rest:
Give us that Peace, O Lord,
    Divine and blest,
Thou keepest for those hearts who love Thee best.
      —*Adelaide A. Procter.*

He that dwelleth in the aid of the Most High shall abide under the protection of the God of Jacob ... He will overshadow thee with His shoulders, and under His wings thou shalt trust. His truth shall compass thee with a shield; thou shalt not be afraid of the terror of the night.... For He hath given His angels charge over thee, to keep thee in all thy ways.
—*Ps. xc. 1, 4, 5, 11.*

* * *

O Lord, my best desires fulfil,
   And help me to resign
Life, health, and comfort, to Thy will,
   And make Thy pleasure mine.
—*Cowper.*

* * *

How beauteous is the courage which we find
With childlike confidence in God combined!
Who fears his God shall know no other fear—
He heeds not pitying smile, nor unkind sneer.

* * *

Onward he moves to meet his latter end,
Angels around befriending virtue's friend;
Sinks to the grave with unperceived decay,

While resignation gently slopes the way;
And all his prospects, brightening to the last,
His heaven commences ere the world is past.
—*Goldsmith.*

LIFE, A CONTINUAL PRAYER

St. Ignatius tells us that it ought to be a familiar practice with us to see God present in everything, and not to wait for the time of prayer to raise our souls toward heaven, but to make our life a continual prayer, so that we find no less devotion in any work of charity and obedience than we do in prayer itself; for every one of our actions ought to be performed solely for the love and service of God.

When St. Teresa had been thinking that her life would be less full of failings if she gave up some external works, Our Lord said, "Courage, it cannot be otherwise; endeavor thou always, in everything to have a right intention, and to look at Me"

To live in the presence of God, and to breathe the atmosphere of prayer are unmistakable marks of "a life hid with Christ in God."

Every day of your life persevere in prayer; for if you neglect this duty, you will be like a soldier going into battle without his weapons—a mere target for the enemy.

HEAVEN

The inspired word assures me that 'it hath not entered into the heart of man to conceive what God has prepared for them that love Him." If no human heart can conceive the happiness of the face-to-face vision of God, still less can a man hope to express this joy in terms of language.

When the divine Infant stood with His little bare feet on Mary's hands in her lap, and put His little arms around her neck, smothering her with His baby kisses—that for Mary was heaven.

When the Baptist heard the Bridegroom's voice ringing joy-bells in his heart and uttering his praise—that for the Baptist was heaven.

When the Beloved Disciple bowed his head, and leaned on the Sacred Heart of his beautiful Jesus—that for John was heaven.

When the Magdalen, all broken at the feet of Jesus, drank in His love and heard her cause so sweetly, so eloquently, so triumphantly advocated—that for her was heaven.

But, then, these lovely experiences were no sooner touched than they vanished, just sips, tastes of heavenly sweetness! All of us have had some passing foretaste of this banquet in store for our souls. A foretaste of this foretaste is, to my thinking, some such heavenly friendship as existed, say, between Scholastica and Benedict, Bernard and Gerard de Chantal, and Francis and Clare of Assisi. Such a friendship is a foretaste of that which is the real foretaste of heaven—intimate and familiar friendship with our dear Lord and Master, Jesus Christ; feeding the hunger of the mind on His thoughts, His character, slaking the thirst of the heart on the torrents of His beautiful love, holding, possessing, and forever enjoying His enchanting company.

MATER DOLOROSA

SUFFERING

There are many who say, 'Why should I suffer? What have I done?" When I hear remarks of that kind I answer: "Are you a Christian man—a follower of Him Who said, 'Deny yourselves, take up your cross, and follow Me'?" Then take up your cross bravely, patiently, and gladly.

Suffering is needed in this world in order that we may develop character. If borne in conformity to the will of God, it brings out all that is good in us, for until we meet with trouble and trial and temptation, sadness, sickness, and sorrow, we have not put forth our whole powers to account. God sends us suffering that its purging fires may purify and make beautiful the Christian soul. But, remember, it will be when we reach that land where death and sorrow shall be no more, and not before, that God will wipe away all tears from our eyes. It is as though He would tell us in His own gentle way that till we reach that life of eternal happiness, tears must furrow our cheeks, and sorrow must be with us, and through a mist of tears, like the haze on the river, the cloud on the mountain, the dew on the heather, we must look up to our home in heaven.

OUR ETERNAL HOME

Only be faithful to your mission in life, be up and doing, true to yourselves, loyal to your country, loving to your God, then the morning of that eternal day will break, when, the curtains of night being flung back, you will stand like Alpine climbers on the mountain top, and see through the golden gates of your Father's house of many mansions the radiant glory of the sun of justice. Then, but not till then, will you drink in the plenitude of immutable life, of immutable truth, of immutable love, and of immutable strength, and the riddle of life will be solved—you will look back upon the trials and troubles, the sickness and the sadness of your earthly pilgrimage, as leaders of armies look back upon their struggles and wounds after the shouts of victory proclaim the battle won.

– Father Bernard Vaughan, S.J.

TRUST AND REST
Confido et Conquiesco

Fret not, poor soul, while doubt and fear
    Disturb thy breast;
The pitying angels, who can see
How vain thy wild regret must be,
    Say, "Trust and rest."

Plan not, nor scheme—but calmly wait;
    His choice is best:
While blind and erring is thy sight,
His wisdom sees and judges right;
    So trust and rest.

Strive not, nor struggle; thy poor might
    Can never wrest
The meanest thing to serve thy will;
All power is His alone; be still,
    And trust and rest.

Desire not; self-love is strong
    Within thy breast;
And yet, He loves thee better still,
So let Him do His loving will—
    And trust and rest.

What dost thou fear? His wisdom reigns
    Supreme confessed:
His power is infinite; His love
Thy deepest, fondest dreams above—
    So trust and rest.

    —*Adelaide A. Procter.*

A GREAT SECRET FOR PRESERVING PEACE OF HEART

A great secret for preserving peace of heart is to do nothing with over-eagerness, but to act always calmly, without disquiet. We are not asked to do much, but to do well. At the *Last Day* God will not examine whether we have performed a multitude of works, but whether we have sanctified our souls in doing them. Now the means of sanctifying ourselves is to do everything for God and to do perfectly whatever we have to do. . The works that have as their motive vanity or selfishness make us neither better nor happier, and we shall receive no reward for them.

Happiness, as it can exist here below, consists in peace, in the joy of a good conscience. Our conscience will be joyous and peaceful if it know not remorse; it will not know remorse if we are careful not to offend God. To fly from sin is, therefore, the chief source of happiness on earth. If our conscience is pure, our life will be happy. There are none happier than saints, for there are none more innocent.

Let us do good; let us avoid evil, and we shall be happy. "There is but one way," said a man of genius, "of being happy, and it is to do well all one's duties."

To continually maintain your peace of soul, keep in mind the presence of God, and do all things to please Him. Think also of your good Guardian Angel who is ever at your side; it will help you to avoid what is wrong and to preserve your equanimity.

ONE LITTLE SECRET OF A HAPPY LIFE

One secret of a sweet and happy Christian life is learning to live by the day. It is the long stretches that tire us. We think of life as a whole, running on for us. We cannot carry this load until we are threescore and ten. We cannot fight this battle continually for half a century. But really there are no long stretches. Life does not come to us all at one time; it comes only a day at a time. Even tomorrow is never ours until it becomes to-day, and we have nothing whatever to do with it but to pass down to it a fair and good inheritance in to-day's work well done, and to-day's life well lived.

It is a blessed secret this, of living by the day. Any one can carry his burden, however heavy, till nightfall. Any one can do his work, however hard, for one day. Any one can live sweetly, patiently, lovingly, purely, until the sun goes down. And this is all life ever means to us—just one little day. "Do to-day's duty; fight to-days temptations, and do not weaken or distract yourself by looking forward to things you cannot see, and could not understand if you saw them." God gives us nights to shut down upon our little days. We cannot see beyond. Short horizons make life easier and give us one of the blessed secrets of brave, true, holy living.

LORD, STAY WITH US

STAY WITH ME, LORD

Stay with me, Lord, the daylight fades,
And slowly fall the purple shades
On mount, on vale, on sunlit glades,
    Stay with me, Lord.

Stay with me, Lord, my day's work is done.
Its busy course is almost run,
Behind the hill-tops sinks the sun,
    Stay with me, Lord.

Stay with me, Lord, I fain would rest
My weary head on Thy dear Breast,
My tender Host, my welcome Guest,
    Stay with me, Lord.

Stay with me, Lord, and ne'er depart,
Hold me to Thee by Love's sweet art,
Keep me within Thy Sacred Heart
    Forever, Lord.

EJACULATIONS FOR A HAPPY DEATH

Jesus, Mary, Joseph, I give you my heart and my soul.

Jesus, Mary, Joseph, assist me in my last agony.

Jesus, Mary, Joseph, may I breathe forth my soul in peace with you.

**MAY ALMIGHTY GOD, THE FATHER,
AND THE SON, AND THE HOLY GHOST
BLESS US.**

* * *

May He support us all the day long, till the shades lengthen, and the evening comes, and the busy world is hushed, and the fever of life is over, and our work is done! Then in His mercy may He give us a safe lodging, and a holy rest, and peace at the last!

—*Cardinal Newman.*

AN ACT OF CONFIDENCE IN GOD

By Blessed Claude de la Colombière, S.J.

My God! I believe so firmly that Thou watchest over all who hope in Thee, and that we can want for nothing when we rely upon Thee in all things, that I am resolved for the future to have no anxieties, and to cast all my cares upon Thee.

* * *

"In peace in the self-same I will sleep and I will rest; for Thou, O Lord, singularly hast settled me in hope."

Men may deprive me of worldly goods and of honors; sickness may take from me my strength and the means of serving Thee; I may even lose Thy grace by sin; but my trust shall never leave me. I will preserve it to the last moment of my life, and the powers of hell shall seek in vain to wrest it from me. *"In peace in the self-same I will sleep and I will rest."*

Let others seek happiness in their wealth, in their talents: let them trust to the purity of their lives, the severity of their mortifications, to the number of their good works, the fervor of their prayers; as for me, O my God, in my very confidence lies all my hope. *"For Thou, O Lord, singularly hast settled me in hope."* This confidence can never be vain. *"No one has hoped in the Lord and has been confounded"*

I am assured, therefore, of my eternal happiness, for I firmly hope for it, and all my hope is in Thee. *"In Thee, O Lord, have I hoped; let me never be confounded."*

I know, alas! I know but too well that I am frail and changeable; I know the power of temptation against the strongest virtue. I have seen stars fall from heaven, and pillars of the firmament totter; but these things alarm me not. While I hope in Thee I am sheltered from all misfortune, and I am sure that my trust shall endure, for I rely upon Thee to sustain this unfailing hope.

Finally, I know that my confidence can not exceed Thy bounty, and that I shall never receive less than I have hoped for from Thee. Therefore I hope that Thou wilt sustain me against my evil inclinations; that Thou wilt protect me against the most furious assaults of the evil one, and that Thou wilt cause my weakness to triumph over my most powerful enemies. I hope that Thou wilt never cease to love me, and that I shall love Thee unceasingly. *"In Thee, O Lord, have I hoped; let me never be confounded."*

The light of Thy countenance, O Lord, is signed upon us: Thou hast given gladness in my heart.

In peace in the self-same; I will sleep and I will rest.

For Thou, O Lord, alone, hast established me in hope (Psalm iv. 8, 10, 11).

AN AFTER-THOUGHT

"Oh! keep me close to Thee," I prayed
  One blest communion morn,
When, tabernacled in my heart,
  Was Christ, my Lord, re-born;

And afterward the meaning
  Of these words came to me,
"What is it, dearest Lord,' I said,
  "To be kept near to Thee?"

Near Thee in lowly Bethlehem,
  In Egypt's exile drear,
In Nazareth's sweet hidden home,
  Each holy silent year;
Near Thee in lone Gethsemani,
  In Thy dread agony,
And all along Thy sorrow's way,
  Even to Calvary.

EJACULATION

O Jesus Christ, Son of the living God, Light of the world, I adore Thee; for Thee I live, for Thee I die. Amen.

Indulgence: 100 days, once a day.—Pius X, July 1, 1909.

* * *

Praised be Jesus Christ forevermore!

SET UP, PRINTED AND BOUND BY BENZIGER BROTHERS, NEW YORK